— BEARS OF THE WORLD —
PANDA BEARS

MARY AUSTEN

PowerKiDS press

New York

Published in 2017 by The Rosen Publishing Group, Inc.
29 East 21st Street, New York, NY 10010

Copyright © 2017 by The Rosen Publishing Group, Inc.

All rights reserved. No part of this book may be reproduced in any form without permission in writing from the publisher, except by a reviewer.

First Edition

Editor: Katie Kawa
Book Design: Reann Nye

Photo Credits: Cover, p. 1 OTHK/Asia Images/Getty Images; cover, pp. 1, 3–24 (background) eva_mask/Shutterstock.com; pp. 4, 18 Eric Isselee/Shutterstock.com; pp. 5, 9, 14, 20, 22 Hung Chung Chih/Shutterstock.com; p. 6 (bamboo) cameilia/Shutterstock.com; p. 6 (panda) anekoho/Shutterstock.com; p. 7 Radu Bercan/Shutterstock.com; pp. 8, 13 leungchopan/Shutterstock.com; p. 10 Sergey Nechaev/Shutterstock.com; p. 11 omepl1/Shutterstock.com; p. 12 ex0rzist/Shutterstock.com; p. 15 Volt Collection/Shutterstock.com; p. 16 Ondrej Prosicky/Shutterstock.com; pp. 17, 19 Keren Su/China Span/Getty Images; p. 21 The Washington Post/Getty Images.

Cataloging-in-Publication Data

Names: Austen, Mary.
Title: Panda bears / Mary Austen.
Description: New York : PowerKids Press, 2017. | Series: Bears of the world | Includes index.
Identifiers: ISBN 9781508149545 (pbk.) | ISBN 9781499420401 (library bound) | ISBN 9781499420395 (6 pack)
Subjects: LCSH: Giant panda–Juvenile literature.
Classification: LCC QL737.C214 A97 2017 | DDC 599.789–d23

Manufactured in the United States of America

CPSIA Compliance Information: Batch #BS16PK: For Further Information contact Rosen Publishing, New York, New York at 1-800-237-9932

CONTENTS

A RARE BEAR 4
LIFE IN THE MOUNTAINS 6
EATING ALL DAY 8
BUILT FOR BAMBOO 10
A CLOSER LOOK 12
ON THE MOVE 14
BABY PANDA BEARS 16
POPULATION PROBLEMS 18
PROTECTING PANDAS 20
LOVED AROUND THE WORLD .22
GLOSSARY 23
INDEX 24
WEBSITES 24

A RARE BEAR

Panda bears are a **rare** kind of bear. These bears, which are commonly known as giant pandas, are found in the wild only in small areas of China. The only other place they can be seen and studied is in zoos around the world.

Pandas are an endangered species, or a kind of animal at risk of dying out. It's believed there are fewer than 2,000 giant pandas alive in the wild today. However, people are working hard to **protect** giant pandas and teach others about these beautiful bears.

raccoon

—Bear Basics—

For a time, people weren't sure if giant pandas were more closely **related** to raccoons or bears. Now, they believe giant pandas are more like bears than they're like any other kind of animal. This is why we sometimes call them panda bears.

Giant pandas are popular zoo animals because many people think they're cute! Some zoos even have "panda cams" that allow you to watch their giant pandas from your computer or smartphone.

LIFE IN THE MOUNTAINS

At one time, giant pandas lived throughout a large part of China and other areas of eastern Asia. Then, people began to clear forests for farmland and building projects, and there wasn't much land left for giant pandas.

Now, giant pandas live in forests high in the mountains of central China. These forests are often cool and wet, which is good weather for these bears. Bamboo plants grow in the forests where giant pandas live. Bamboo is a kind of tall, woody grass with a **hollow** stem.

bamboo

GIANT PANDAS IN THE WILD

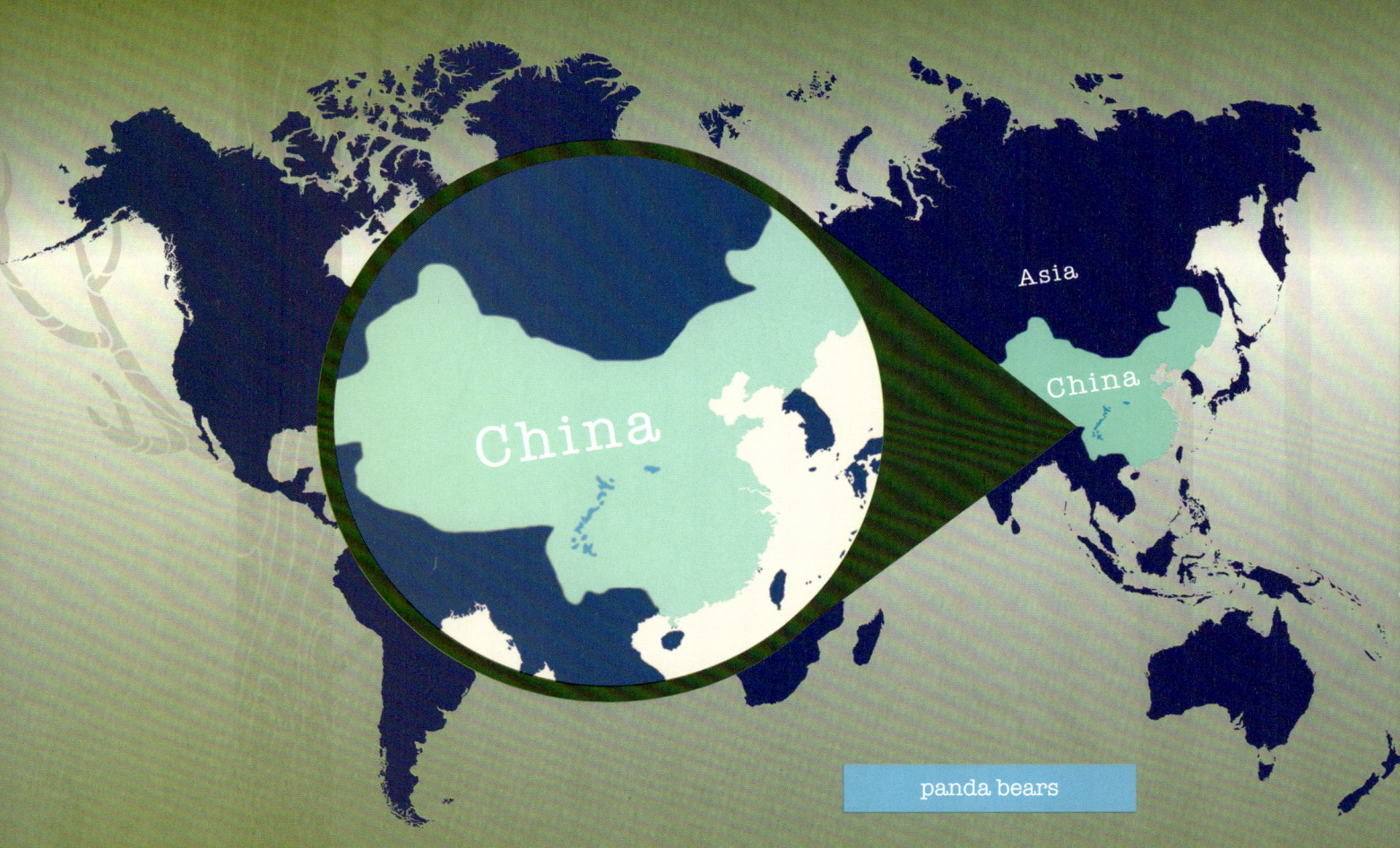

panda bears

This map shows where giant pandas are found in the wild. These bears need to live in bamboo forests because bamboo makes up a large part of their daily diet, or the food they eat.

7

EATING ALL DAY

A giant panda eats almost nothing but bamboo. This plant makes up as much as 99 percent of a giant panda's diet. Giant pandas eat bamboo stems, leaves, and shoots.

Bamboo is easy for giant pandas to find, but it doesn't have a lot of **nutrients**. A giant panda's digestive system, or the part of its body that breaks down food, can't break down certain parts of this plant. To make up for these problems, giant pandas eat huge amounts of bamboo. They can eat for as many as 16 hours each day!

— Bear Basics —

A giant panda's digestive system can't break down parts of bamboo because it's meant to break down meat. At one time, giant pandas ate more meat than bamboo, and their digestive system didn't change when their diet did.

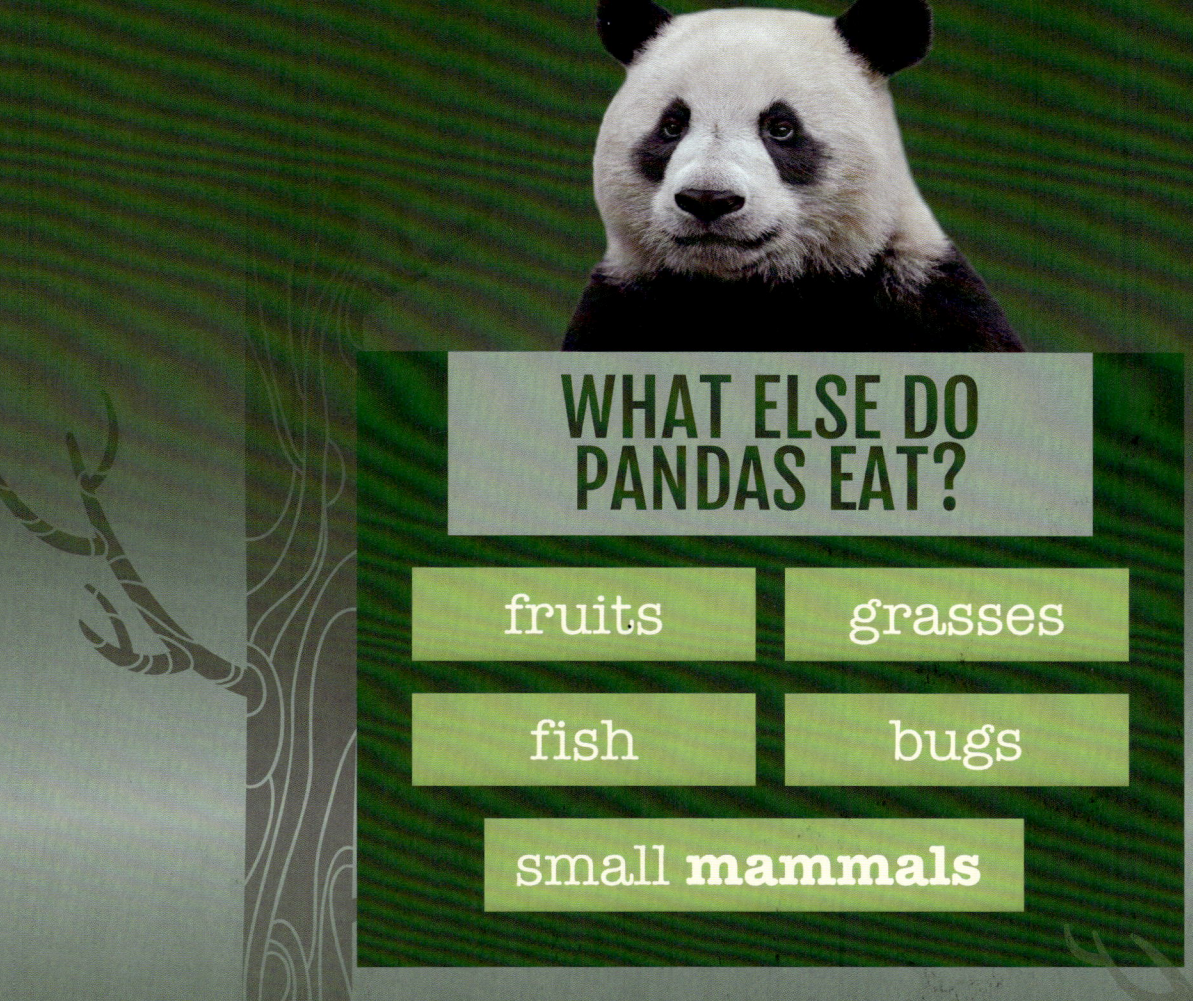

WHAT ELSE DO PANDAS EAT?

- fruits
- grasses
- fish
- bugs
- small **mammals**

Although giant pandas mainly eat bamboo, they're still considered omnivores. This means they eat both plants and animals. These are some of the other things a giant panda might eat in the wild.

BUILT FOR BAMBOO

Giant pandas have certain **adaptations** that help them eat as much bamboo as possible. Many of their teeth are wide and have **ridges**, which makes them good for chewing tough bamboo plants.

Giant pandas have also learned to eat while sitting upright. This makes them look like a person sitting on the ground. Sitting this way allows a giant panda to use its front paws to hold the bamboo it's eating. It holds bamboo with the help of a longer wristbone covered with a pad of skin that acts like a person's thumb.

A giant panda needs to eat more than 20 pounds (9.1 kg) of bamboo each day.

A CLOSER LOOK

Giant pandas have earned their name! They're large mammals that can weigh more than 250 pounds (113.4 kg). Giant pandas are most often between 4 and 6 feet (1.2 and 1.8 m) long. Male giant pandas are generally larger than females. Both males and females have a round head.

Giant pandas are known for the colors of their fur. They have black fur on their ears, arms, legs, and shoulders, as well as around their eyes. The rest of their body is covered with white fur.

A giant panda's thick fur keeps it warm in the cool mountain forests it calls home.

ON THE MOVE

Giant pandas spend most of their time eating or sleeping. This has caused some people to think these bears can't move around very well. However, giant pandas are actually good at climbing trees and swimming.

Unlike many other bears, giant pandas don't go into a deep sleep during winter. Instead, they often travel from higher parts of the mountains to lower areas when it gets colder. Giant pandas are generally solitary animals. This means they mainly live alone.

—Bear Basics—
Giant pandas send messages to each other by leaving their scent on trees, grass, and rocks. They can also make sounds such as a growl.

Giant pandas are large animals, but they're good at climbing trees.

BABY PANDA BEARS

While giant pandas are on their own most of the time, things change during the mating season. This is the time of year when male and female giant pandas come together to make babies. The mating season for giant pandas lasts from March to May.

Female giant pandas often have two babies, or cubs, at once, but they can only care for one. This means the other baby is left to die. When giant pandas are born, they're not "giant" at all. In fact, they're only about as big as a stick of butter!

—Bear Basics—

Some people who study giant pandas believe these bears might not be as solitary as we once thought. They think giant pandas sometimes come together in the wild during times other than the mating season.

Giant pandas are born blind. It can take up to eight weeks for a giant panda cub to open its eyes for the first time.

POPULATION PROBLEMS

A giant panda cub stays with its mother for at least a year after it's born. Sometimes it stays with its mother for up to three years! Until a cub leaves to live on its own, a mother giant panda can't have more cubs. This has made it hard for the wild giant panda population to grow.

Male and female pandas don't mate often in zoos. People who study pandas are trying to figure out the reasons for this in order to help these bears reproduce, or make more bears.

Female giant pandas can only mate and have a baby at certain times each year. This makes it hard for the population of this endangered species to grow in the wild and in zoos.

PROTECTING PANDAS

Giant pandas have few natural predators. Some animals, such as the yellow-throated marten, hunt panda cubs, but adult pandas generally aren't hunted by other animals. However, people sometimes still illegally hunt these bears for their fur. This kind of illegal hunting is called poaching. Giant pandas are also in danger of losing more of the bamboo forests where they live because of human activity.

People around the world are working to protect giant pandas. Reserves, or protected areas of land, have been created in China for these bears. Zoos have also **provided** a safe home for giant pandas.

— Bear Basics —
It's believed there are around 300 giant pandas living in zoos and breeding, or mating, centers around the world.

People who work at zoos and breeding centers take good care of giant pandas so these bears live long and healthy lives.

LOVED AROUND THE WORLD

Giant pandas are only found in the wild in a small area of one country. However, they're loved by people around the world. Many people travel to see giant pandas in zoos or enjoy looking at pictures of them in the wild.

Giant pandas are hard to **observe** in the wild, so zoos and breeding centers make it easier to study these bears. The things people have learned in these places are being used to help save this endangered species. The number of pandas in the wild is on the rise!

GLOSSARY

adaptation: A change in a living thing that helps it live better in its habitat.

hollow: Having empty space inside.

mammal: Any warm-blooded animal whose babies drink milk and whose body is covered with hair or fur.

nutrient: Something taken in by a plant or animal that helps it grow and stay healthy.

observe: To look at something closely.

protect: To keep safe.

provide: To supply for use.

rare: Not seen often.

related: Belonging to the same group or family because of shared qualities.

ridge: A raised part or area.

INDEX

A
Asia, 6, 7

B
bamboo, 6, 7, 8, 9, 10, 11, 20
breeding centers, 20, 21, 22

C
China, 4, 6, 7, 20
cubs, 16, 17, 18, 20

D
diet, 7, 8
digestive system, 8

E
endangered species, 4, 18, 22

F
forests, 6, 7, 13, 20
fur, 12, 13, 20

G
grass, 6, 9, 14

M
mammals, 9, 12
mating season, 16
mountains, 6, 13, 14

P
paws, 10
poaching, 20
predators, 20

R
raccoons, 4
reserves, 20

S
solitary, 14, 16

T
teeth, 10

W
winter, 14

Y
yellow-throated marten, 20

Z
zoos, 4, 5, 18, 20, 21, 22

WEBSITES

Due to the changing nature of Internet links, PowerKids Press has developed an online list of websites related to the subject of this book. This site is updated regularly. Please use this link to access the list: www.powerkidslinks.com/bworld/panda